What Do You See?

A Children's Book About Diversity, Inclusion and Black History

JERYN ALISE TURNER

HIGGINS PUBLISHING
DALLAS, TEXAS

Published by Higgins Publishing. All rights reserved.
Copyright 2022 * Jeryn Alise Turner * What Do You See? A Children's Book About Diversity, Inclusion and Black History

Higgins Publishing supports the rights to free expression and the value of copyright. The purpose of copyright is to encourage writers and artists to produce creative works that enrich our values. The scanning, uploading, and distribution of this book without the express permission of the publisher is a theft of intellectual property. If you would like permission to use material from this book (other than for review purposes), please contact permissions@higginspublishing.com. Thank you for your support of copyright law.

Higgins Publishing | www.higginspublishing.com - The publisher is not responsible for websites (or their content) that are not owned by the publisher. Higgins Publishing is committed to excellence in the publishing industry. The company reflects the philosophy established by the founder, based on Psalm 68:11, "The Lord gave the word, and great was the company of those who published it."

Library of Congress Control Number: 2022920565
Pages cm. 48   February 2023
Higgins Publishing 1st Edition
What Do You See? A Children's Book About Diversity, Inclusion and Black History
Turner, Jeryn Alise

ISBN Numbers:
978-1-941580-39-4 (HB) * 978-1-941580-38-7 (PB) * 978-1-041-580-37-0 (EB)

- Young Adult Fiction / Social Themes / Self-Esteem & Self-Reliance
- Young Adult Fiction / Social Themes / Emotions & Feelings
- Young Adult Fiction / Diversity & Multicultural
- Social Science / Holiday (Non-Religious)
- Young Adult Non-Fiction/ Social Themes / Self-Esteem & Self-Reliance Ballerina Firsts

African-American Ballerinas Black History Firsts Trivia
- Young Adult Non-Fiction / Social Themes / Self-Esteem & Self-Reliance

For information about special discounts for bulk purchases, subsidiary rights, foreign and translations rights, or fundraising, contact Higgins Publishing at contact@higginspublishing.com.

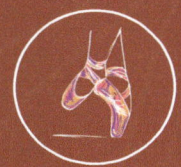

DEDICATION

I dedicate this book to my niece who teaches me courage and other brave souls who are not afraid to try new things or be the only. Embrace your fearless spirit and never be afraid to do what you are inspired to do.

~

To Women who are United, On the Come Up, and Never Afraid to Be First. A concept driving the work and innovation of FRH Golden. Adam 'FRH' Golden is an accomplished entrepreneur and recording artist who is committed to empowerment. He uses his platform to promote community upliftment and freedom of expression.

To learn more about FRH Golden, go to https://frhmarket.com

I am so excited - it's my first day
at the performing arts school!!!!
Outfits picked out,
I am ready to learn all the new rules

Will people know me and will they speak???
Will I have things in common
with the kids I meet??

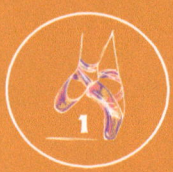

Mom took me to Princess Hair Salon,
they braided my hair
It has to be extra special
because this year I really care

I need to look good;
the school goes up to twelfth grade!
Usually confident,
why am I questioning decisions I've made?

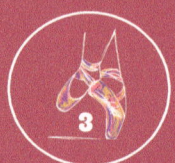

Never stop dreaming, you are our dream.

Afro Queen

My grandmother Gigi took me shopping,
I have cool gear
Although I feel really nervous,
I won't show any fear

As a dancer, my first class is ballet,
it gives me a chance to move
Even though I am new,
hopefully there's nothing I need to prove

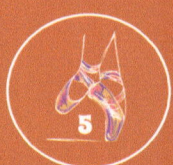

When I walk into the class
all eyes are on me
Which makes me stop and think,
what do they really see?

Is it my hair? It looks different -
I usually wear it curly
Is it my style?
I love to wear sneakers
and not too girly

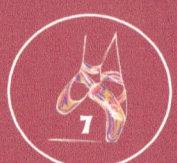

Is it my silliness?
Everyone is acting so much older
Is it my competitiveness?
This year I want to be bolder

Everything feels so strange,
things aren't the same
When I introduce myself,
people ask about my name

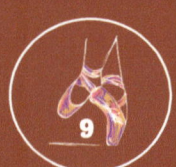

"Where does it come from?
I've never heard it before"
It's African and means "to manifest more"

I wanted to see my friends
and hoped we would get together
But things still feel really weird
whenever we gather…

Masks are still a thing;
I pause before I hug my friends
Homemade snacks and cookies,
mom no longer sends

Everywhere we go
still has signs up about COVID
I am over it and I wish
we could just go back to being kids

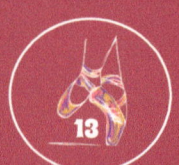

Today, we have an assembly
and are forced to spread out
No one knows the topic;
we are wondering what it's about

Just at that moment,
my principal walks to the microphone
There are other teachers behind her,
but she's standing alone

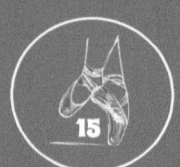

When we walk into the auditorium,
there are pictures everywhere
I have seen these pictures before,
but the other kids stare

I smile when I see a picture of Maya Angelou
As I look at other Black leaders
I wonder what we will do

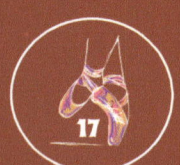

She waits for the noise to stop
before beginning to speak
She introduces herself as Ms. Griffin
and wishes us a good week

Everyone looks shocked!
Are we really doing work on the first day?
She then asks us to think about everything
that is happening today

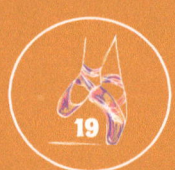

As she says this, I remember a few things at home
that felt really weird
If the news was on, the channel quickly changed;
the image disappeared

My mom was more upset than usual,
but I didn't understand why
So, I decided to ask her what was going on,
and she let out a sigh

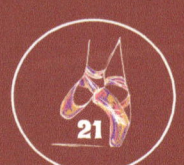

Mom told me that some bad people
were unfairly treating others
And, sadly, the people being hurt
looked like her sister and brother

Unfortunately, this treatment was
really harsh and people died
And because these people reminded her
of our family, she cried

In response, people began to protest and marched
peacefully in the street
Which made me think of Rosa Parks
when she didn't give up her seat

My principal points to an image and asks
when this picture was taken
We don't raise our hands because
we are confused and a bit shaken

The principal asks us to look closer,
and we see the clothes look new
She says perspective and opinion changes
depending on our view

What one person sees another may overlook
based on how he/she reacts
But the purpose of education is to
rely less on opinion and teach facts

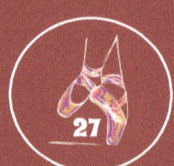

She asks us to look closely and reexamine
the images of the pictures we see
Then asks us to identify the differences
but also focus on finding similarities

I study the images and recognize Mother Theresa
and Gandhi and a few more
Reminds me of FRH market where empowerment
is the focus of my uncle's online store

11:11 AM

Stacey Abrams

Gandhi

Mother Theresa

Maya Angelou

Jane Fonda

Finally, one of the older boys raises his hand
and says we all want peace
The principal urges us to continue to talk
and work together so injustices can cease

Because of their sacrifice and bravery,
the equality display will stay up
Reminding us of past and recent events
that caused conflict to erupt

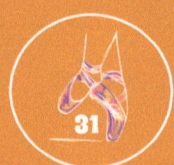

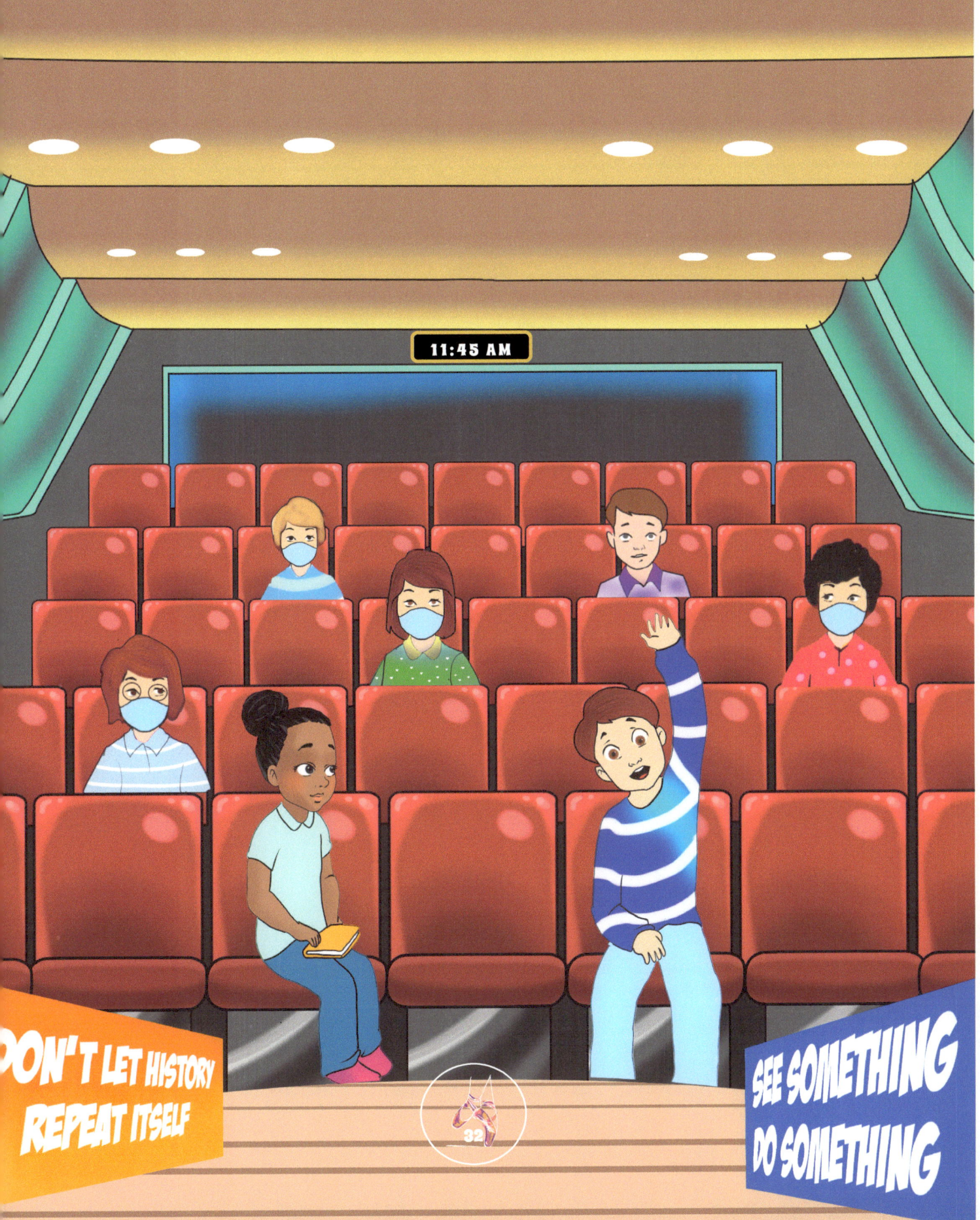

She said it is easy to see race
and assume differences will divide
But much better to see people as individuals
and let that be your guide

As I sit in my chair and think about the question
of what others see
I hope style, humor and dance skills
are what people remember about me

As I walk to my locker to get my books,
I am thinking about what Ms. Griffin said
With all that I just heard, is racism better now
than in the Ruby Bridges story we read?

My friends all look and act differently,
but what if we are the exception and not the rule
And what if our friendship changes
now that we are in different programs at school?

The day is finally over, and as I walk outside
to get picked up I look around
The street is full of activity: kids talking,
horns beeping, so many city sounds

While I wait, I think about this new school
and what Ms. Griffin had to say
With everything changing around me and in my life,
I just hope I will be okay...

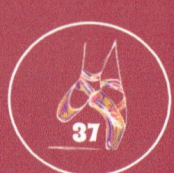

African-American Ballerinas
Black History Firsts Trivia

Find the year of accomplishment for each ballerina listed and write what you find in the **What Do You See? Creative Coloring Book Companion Journal** For Kids About Black History Firsts, Diversity and Inclusion. Scan the QR Code to get yours today!

Precious Adams — Joined the English National Ballet, and was promoted to First Artist.

Olivia Boisson — The First African-American woman to join the Corps De Ballet of the New York City Ballet in over a decade.

Lauren Anderson — The First African-American principal dancer of the Houston Ballet.

Karen Brown — The First African-American woman to direct a ballet company when she served as artistic director of Oakland Ballet Company in California.

Aesha Ash — Founded the Swan Dream Project to encourage African-American children to start ballet.

Janet Collins — The First African-American prima ballerina with the Metropolitan Opera.

Debra Austin — The First African-American woman to join the prestigious New York City Ballet.

Misty Copeland — The First African-American female principal dancer in American Ballet Theatre's 75-year history.

These Ballerinas Made Their Mark For You And Generations To Come!!!

~~~

Chrystyn Fentroy — Principal dancer with Boston Ballet.

Sydney Magruder Washington — Ballet dancer and mental health advocate.

Michaela DePrince — Featured in the ballet documentary First Position.

Anne Benna Sims — The First African-American woman to hold a contract with the American Ballet Theatre.

Virginia Johnson — Founding company member and prima ballerina of Dance Theatre of Harlem.

Llanchie Stevenson — The First African-American dancer at Radio City Music Hall Ballet Company.

Alicia Graf Mack — The First woman of color and youngest person to hold the director of dance division at Julliard.

Raven Wilkinson — One of the First African-American ballerinas allowed to join a ballet company.

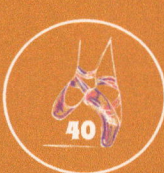

Epilogue

As we all learn to navigate new chapters in our lives,
I encourage you to be tenacious and
relentless in pursuing your dreams.

May we all remember that no matter what, we are
braver than we think and stronger
than we can ever imagine.

Thank You For Your Purchase!

~~~

If you enjoyed this book, please post a review
where you purchased this book,
or scan the QR Code to post a review at Amazon.

Ballerina Firsts Reference Key

Clark Hine, Darlene (ed.), Black Women in America: An Historical Encyclopedia, Vols 1 and 2, New York: Carlson Publishing, 1993.

Dunning, Jennifer. "Janet Collins, 86: Ballerina Was First Black Artist at Met Opera." The New York Times, May 31, 2003.

"Pioneering dancer proves her point(e) " by Martha Quillin, The News & Observer, July 13, 2016

Bartók No. 3, New York City Ballet

"The Ballet: Bartok No.3 by Clive Barnes, The New York Times, May 25, 1974

Kourlas, Gia (May 6, 2007). "Dance: Where Are All the Black Swans?". The New York Times. Retrieved February 22, 2012.

"Llanchie Stevenson – MOBBallet.org". mobballet.org. Retrieved 17 March 2018.

Ferguson, Jill L. (February 19, 2019). "A ballerina who reached her dreams now helps kids reach theirs". The Washington Post.

Kourlas, Gia (August 13, 2020). "Aesha Ash Takes Her Place at the Head of the Class". The New York Times. ISSN 0362-4331.

"Faculty". School of American Ballet. Retrieved August 31, 2020.

"She's on Point: After seven years, ABT ballerina Misty Copeland becomes a soloist". Sixaholic. 2007

Cooper, Michael. "Misty Copeland Is Promoted to Principal Dancer at American Ballet Theater", The New York Times, June 30, 2015. Retrieved June 30, 2015.

Siegal, Nina (13 March 2015). "For Michaela DePrince, a Dream Comes True at the Dutch National Ballet". The New York Times.

https://www.bostonballet.org/Home/Global/Profiles/Artists/Second-Soloists/Michaela-DePrince.aspx | date= 11 December 2021}

"U.S. Ballerina Faces Discrimination at Bolshoi Academy". The Moscow Times. 19 November 2013. Retrieved 8 August 2018.

Faines, Ayesha K. (7 July 2015). "10 Black Ballerinas Other Than Misty Copeland Who Are Also Changing the Face of Ballet". Atlanta Black Star. Retrieved 7 August 2018.

Mackrell, Judith (28 November 2013). "Everyday racism: how to be a black ballet dancer in a white world". The Guardian. Retrieved 8 August 2018.

"Precious Adams". English National Ballet. 21 February 2017. Retrieved 16 April 2020.

"Ballerina Precious Adams explains why she won't wear the traditional pink tights: 'I'm not colourblind". The Independent. September 20, 2018. Archived from the original on 2022-06-14. Retrieved 16 April 2020.

"Black Ballerina Fights Racism to Be the Best", Jet, March 19, 1981, p. 64

"Meet Virginia Johnson: From Prima Ballerina to Dance Theatre of Harlem Artistic Director". Pittsburgh Ballet Theatre. 2017-03-14. Retrieved 2018-03-06.

"Karen Brown". mobballet.org. Retrieved 2019-10-01.

Wood Rudulph, Heather (December 29, 2014). "Get That Life: How I Became a Professional Ballerina". Cosmopolitan.

Kwon, Beth (2006). "Pointe Taken". Columbia Magazine.

Rizvic, Veneta (September 25, 2015). "Alicia Graf Mack discusses challenges in life as a dancer (Video)". St. Louis Business Journal.

King, Susan (March 8, 2013). "Dance Spotlight: Alicia Graf Mack on keeping Alvin Ailey legacy alive". Los Angeles Times.

"Portrait: Alicia Graf Mack". Juilliard School. August 28, 2018. Barone, Joshua (April 10, 2018).

"Juilliard's New Dance Director Comes From Ailey and Ballet". The New York Times.

Holmes, Kathryn (January 2, 2020). "A Day in the Life of Alicia Graf Mack, Head of Juilliard's Dance Division". Dance Teacher.

"Brown Ballerina Spotlight: Q & A Olivia Boisson", July 29, 2015, browngirlsdoballet.com

"What the Dance World Still Gets Wrong About Mental Illness", Dance Magazine, February 1, 2019

"Chrystyn Mariah Fentroy", profile at Boston Ballet.

CPSIA information can be obtained
at www.ICGtesting.com
Printed in the USA
JSHW041006210223
37990JS00001B/7